48 FAMOUS STUDIES
For OBOE or SAXOPHONE
by W. FERLING, Op. 31
Revised by Albert J. Andraud

2

B103

4

6

8

Largo, mesto (92 = ♪)

15

Allegretto risoluto (120 = ♩)

16

① Use the open C♯.

21 Maestoso (108 = ♩)

22 Allo moderato (116 = ♩)

(1)Take the double G# key with the right first finger.

(1) In a fast tempo the high E♭ can be produced by adding the G♯ key to the high D.

Largo lagrimoso (96 = ♪)

27

Allº spiritoso (126 = ♩)

28

(1) Use the open C#.
(2) All through this study the open C# may be used.

Andante con gravita (72 = ♪)

35

Scherzo (80 = ♩.)

36

(1) Use the low C♮-D♭ Trill.

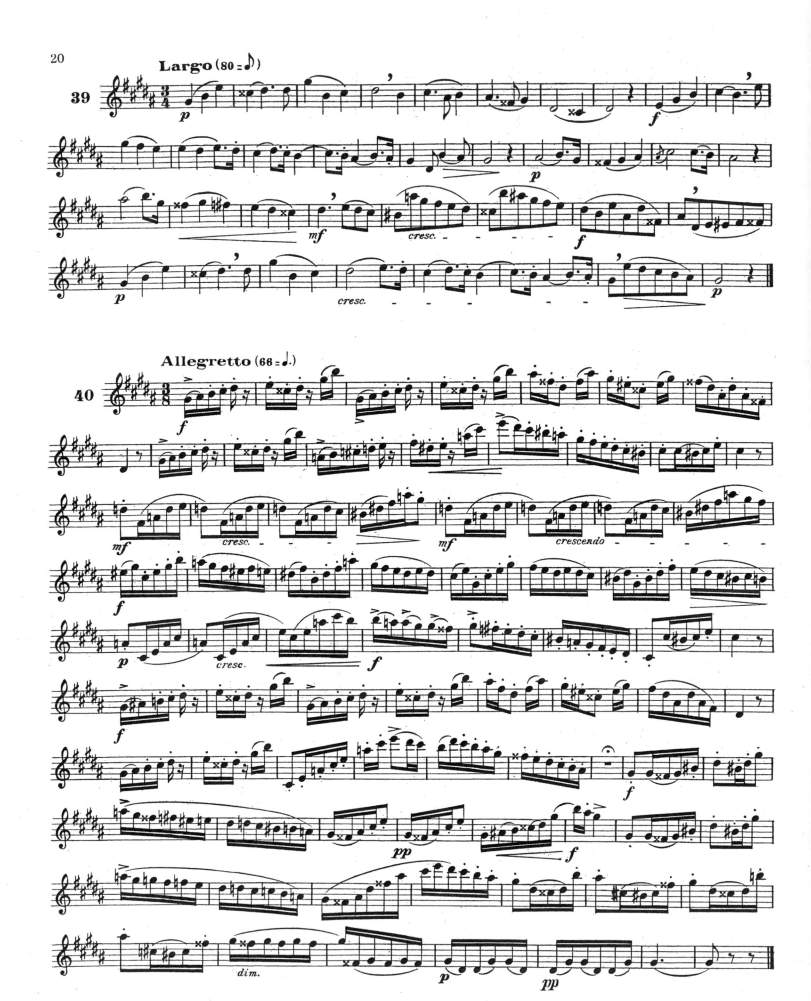

⑴The double E♮ and A♮ keys must be pressed down together with the left little finger.

Marcia funebre (72 = ♪)

43

Tempo di Marcia (126 = ♩)

44

(1) Start this E♭ with the right little finger and then change to the left little finger in order to avoid the awkward sliding from E♭ to D♭.

TROIS DUOS CONCERTANTS

pour deux Hautbois or for TWO SAXOPHONES

W. FERLING.

Op. 13.

OBOE 1.

RONDO.

DUET
No. 2.

Allegro

B103

OBOE 1.

RONDO.—MINUETTO.

Poco vivace.

D.C. al Fine.

TRIO

for Two Oboes and English Horn
Op. 87

1st Oboe

Ludwig van Beethoven
Revised by Albert J. Andraud

1st Oboe

Large notes are Beethoven's original writing.

Menuetto da capo, senza replica e poi la Coda

B103

Finale ♩=168
Presto

May be omitted if cues
in 2nd Oboe are used.

May be omitted.

1st Oboe

Selected Oboe Publications

METHODS

ANDRAUD, ALBERT J.

B412   **Vade Mecum of the Oboist (Grade 3)**   HL3770621
230 selected technical and orchestral studies for the Oboe or English Horn). Compiled and edited by Albert Andraud.

BAERMANN, CARL
Hite, David

B495   **Foundation Studies (Grade 3)**   HL3770806
Scales, chord and intervals for daily practice patterned after Carl Baermann, Op. 63.

FERLING, WILHELM
Andraud, Albert J.

B571   **18 Studies, Op. 12**   HL3770916

B103   **48 Famous Studies, 1st Part (Grade 3)**   HL3770173
These studies have been long established as one of the centerpieces of study repertoire for both the oboe and saxophone.In addition to the 48 famous Ferling studies in includes 3 Duos Concertants for two instruments and Trio for two oboes and English horn by Beethoven. Second oboe/sax part available as 03770175.

B104   **48 Famous Studies, 2nd Part (Grade 3)**   HL3770175
These studies have been long established as one of the centerpieces of study repertoire for both the oboe and saxophone. In addition to the 48 famous Ferling studies in includes 3 Duos Concertants for two instruments and Trio for two oboes and English horn by Beethoven. This is the 2nd part in the series.

HITE, DAVID

B473   **Melodious and Progressive Studies, Bk. 2 (Grade 3)**   HL3770716

COLLECTIONS

HANDEL, GEORGE FRIDERIC
Andraud, Albert J.

B108   **Five Solos (Grade 3)**   HL3770183
I. Famous Largo, II. Concerto in G Minor, III. Sonate I, IV. Sonate II, V. Sonate III

SOLO, UNACCOMPANIED

TELEMANN, GEORG PHILLIPP
Forrest, Sidney

B453   **Fantasies I-XII (1 - 12) (Grade 3)**   HL3770644
The "Twelve Fantasies" are a faithful reflection of the "gallant style" of the age. They were written about 1732, during the height of Telemann's career and faithfully depict his movement away from the Baroque into freer forms, giving an improvisatory and somewhat spontaneous feeling to these works. These solo fantasies of Telemann have been beloved late Baroque works by flutists for centuries. Their beauty and incredible interpretive opportunities are offered to oboists in this wonderful transcription by Sidney Forrest.

SOLO WITH PIANO

BARNES, JAMES

ST578   **Autumn Soliloquy for Oboe and Piano (Grade 3)**   HL3775314
A delightful tone poem composed as an oboe solo with wind orchestra accompaniment and dedicated to Susan Hicks Brashier. Later versions for solo clarinet and flute, and orchestra and band accompaniments followed. Each solo instrument with piano accompaniment is also available for recitals and contest. Grade 3, ca. 7'.

BELLINI, VINCENZO
Peters, Harry

SS934   **Concerto in E Flat (Grade 3)**   HL3774621
Edited by Harry Peters

HANDEL, GEORGE FRIDERIC
Andraud, Albert J.

SS182   **Concerto Grosso No. 8 in B Flat (Grade 3)**   HL3773789

KREISLER, ALEXANDER VON

SS695   **Sonatina (Grade 3)**   HL3774349
Though composed for oboe and piano, Kreisler's Sonatina is also very effective when performed on flute.

TELEMANN, GEORG PHILLIPP
Andraud, Albert J.

SS136   **Sonata in a Minor (Grade 3)**   HL3773739
A four movement sonata, this piece offers the player the opportunity to play in the Baroque style with ornamentations. Movement titles: I. Siciliana: Andante grazioso, II. Spirituoso: Allegretto, III. Andante amabile, IV. Vivace

SS137   **Sonata in g Minor (Grade 3)**   HL3773740
This edition was revised by Albert Andraud, and can be performed on oboe and flute. The piano accompaniment includes Baroque figured bass notation. Movements: I. Grave, II. Alla Breve, III. Adagio, IV. Vivace

TRIO

BEETHOVEN, LUDWIG VAN
Andraud, Albert J.

SS862   **Trio, Op. 87 for Two Oboes and English Horn**   HL3774539
Beethoven's Trio Op. 87 has long been one of the composer's most popular works. This revised edition by Albert Andraud expresses the French romantic tradition of his heritage, providing performers a distinctive approach to this charming classical-style work. Movement titles: 1. Allegro 2. Adagio 3. Menuet and Trio 4. Finale

MCCARTY, EVELYN

B540   **Oboe Duets and Trios, Volume Two (Grade 3)**   HL3770885
Volume 2 of this collection contains 20 country dances originating from Mexico, England, Scotland, Ireland, France, and Spain, all arranged for oboe duets, trios, or two oboes and English Horn. They can be performed by the amateur or the connoisseur, and the players will find these dances varies and expressive. Songs included: 1. The Contra Rigaudon, 2. The Spanish Flag, 3. The Drunken Peasant, 4. Today's Vanities, 5. The Kelston's House, 6. The Molinet, 7. The Surrender, 8. The Cock, 9. The Gypsy's March, 10. The Crazy Ones, 11. Jacques, 12. The Girl from Hamburg, 13. The Amah's Pearl, 14. The Pill (A Whimsey), 15. Bartolito, 16. Stately March, 17. The Devil had his Night, 18. The Emblem of the Abbey, 19. Pavane, 20. The Beaux Stratagem

Exclusively distributed by  HAL•LEONARD® CORPORATION

Questions/ comments? info@laurenkeisermusic.com